So Before I Let You Go

So Before I Let You Go

THOUGHT CATALOG

THOUGHT
CATALOG
Books

BROOKLYN, NY

Cover photography by © Kristopher Roller, Designed by KJ Parish.

Published by Thought Catalog Books, a publishing house owned by The Thought & Expression Co., Williamsburg, Brooklyn.

First edition, 2017

ISBN: 978-1974634774

Printed and bound in the United States.

10 9 8 7 6 5 4 3 2 1

Contents

How To Find The Art Of Letting Go

Kathleen-June Horne

When faced with pain two roads stretch out before you, each begging you to hurtle yourself down it in an attempt to let go of, to escape, the emotions that threaten to consume your very being. The first is a negative, sorrowful road full of heartbreak and dulled tears, whilst the second is a wistfully nostalgic road littered with *maybes* and *perhaps* that never fully bloomed. **Those are the classic types of "letting go", understood by most, revered by few.** In order to elevate this concept to an art, however, the event had to have once been a true part of you, you had to have almost breathed a future, a life, where this significant thing had happened to you. There's the kind of longing after a loss that makes you angry, that seeks vengeance against whatever was taken away from you, but that's merely wounded pride. Soon it will fade, like a bruise, leaving behind no permanent mark or scar. It's the anguished longing that cuts the deepest, leaving you staring up at the blank ceiling at night, with nothing but a twisting heart. It's a kind of pain that never fades, instead, you learn to live with it, to bury it in apathy and turn your head away from couples on the subway because overall, more than anything, it's a feeling of *I can't.* I can't do this, I can't love, I can't feel because each movement is painful and every time I am reminded of what I no longer have my heart freezes a little bit more. It gnaws away at you, piece by piece until your hands begin to shake and the shadows of your face begin to take on a life of their own. You waste away beneath a thundercloud, a torrential downpour you can't begin to understand the ebb and flow of because if you did it wouldn't feel so much like drowning. You feel an oddly pressing sense of claustrophobia even standing in the empty parking lot of a big box store at 3 AM, trying to remember why you're there. But then, one day, as crazy as it seems, as dark and endless and hopeless as it all seemed, the pain begins to leave your body the way snow melts in March. First, it trickles away slowly, but soon all at once, pouring away from you like a waterfall, leaving you baptized in the strength of freedom. In living it you let it go, and in letting go you finally break through to the other side, stronger and wiser than you were before. For, in the end, the art of letting go is indeed an art in that the final goal cannot be seen until it has been completed. Art is flexible, it can become anything, take nearly any amount of time, and will always maintain an innate value because it contains a bit of the artist's soul. The only thing that an art form asks of us is patience, an ability to keep going and understand that the process makes the piece as well as the artist. **That's really letting go**, in that when you have gained something from something there's a kind of power that comes from understanding your worth and pain.

17 Days Of Watching You Fall Out Of Love With Me

Joms Zulueta Jimenez

Day 1

You asked me to cut my hair. At first, I thought you were just joking, but you suddenly gave me a look of a 5-year old kid who doesn't want to eat vegetables and insisted that I should cut it. I remember the first time we met, your eyes were a miner of gold, marveled by my straight long hair and you told me to keep it 'cos it cost an arm and a leg to you.

Day 2

You told me that you were sad, so I left my office early to surprise you with a box of your favorite donuts. Unfortunately, I got stuck in traffic. I told you to wait for me for a couple of minutes because I had something, but…you told me that you were already out with your friends and you asked me to go home instead. I kept my dismay inside the box of a failed surprise hoping that you'd be able to grasp it.

Day 3

You were happy. You were happy because you finally finished the series that you were binge watching. You were happy because you were able to sleep more than 7 hours. You were happy because you made a perfect sunny side up. You were happy because your friend was getting married and when I told you that we would get to that point; you paused and that pause was the loudest rejection I have ever heard.

Day 4

We did not see each other. The first message I received was a "thank you." I was glad that you finally checked the gift I gave you 2 days prior. I replied with a message that rivaled Neruda's poems about love. You replied with a heart emoji. That was then the last message I received from you that day.

Day 5

I asked what was wrong. You answered by asking the same question. I talked turkey while you ran a mile. I couldn't remember the last time you answered in a complete sentence.

Day 6

You spoke in fragments and fillers and verbal nods. Your "good morning" was a flat text written on the wind and your cryptic messages became harder and harder to decipher. It had been a while since the last time I saw your "good night" and lately, I had instead been receiving plain and templated 2-minute phone calls telling me to sleep early or just, "Honey, I'm busy, I'll call you back."

Day 7

Your gestures reminded me of the final days of spring—beautiful but fading—as well as the beginning of winter; cold. When we were together, it felt like a long distance relationship. We were holding hands, but the feeling was empty. I missed you. I missed you so, so badly even though you were just beside me.

Day 8

I cut my hair. I cut my hair with the hopes that it might save us. It sounded like bullshit, I know, but I ran out of reasons why you were aloof or why it seemed like you were half-hearted or why I felt uncomfortable with peace. I cut my hair. You said I looked better. That was a relief.

Day 9

Kissing became awkward to you. Every touch seemed offensive.

Day 10...11, 12, 13, 14

We did not talk.

Day 15

I said sorry. I apologized for something that I wasn't even certain of. I apologized for not initiating a conversation. I apologized for asking for too much of your time. I apologized for being not enough. I didn't want to get used to it, but I didn't want to get rid of it either, so I apologized. *Please.*

Day 16

We were together, but in between your silence and my loneliness, I found closure.

Day 17

We stopped talking and from day one until this day, I knew, it was over.

3

You Left Me With No Closure

Liane White

Sometimes I think about how perfect my life would be if you didn't leave.

It could be a random thought that flickers through my mind as I walk past your house or the places we used to go. My face stares blankly, wordlessly, yet my mind is far from calm.

After all this time, my heart still pounds painfully against my chest at the thought of you.

Sometimes I look at your old messages when I miss you. Your heartfelt encouragement to tell me not to give up, your light-hearted jokes to made me smile, your blind devotion towards me as you thought the world of me, and your steely, unwavering love that made me believe in love.

And on the days I am suddenly overwhelmed with this strong curiosity to know how you are doing, I go to your social media and am bombarded with pictures of you and her. I am reminded, again, of how lacking I am in comparison to her because if I were better, you would have loved me. You wouldn't have left and I wouldn't be left with all the unspoken words and this aching need for you. There wouldn't be a before you and after you version of me.

The demise of us did not happen over time. It was abrupt, sudden, and shocking. And there was nothing I could have done to prevent it.

One moment I was in your arms, dreaming of our future together. The next you sat me down and tried to convince me how there was no way we could be together. We were too different, you tried to explain. I shook my head hoping this was all a nightmare and I would wake up soon to a reality where you were back to your usual self. You were still talking and I didn't want to listen. I couldn't accept what you were saying and for the first time, I wanted to run away from you. I wanted to yell at you and ask, after all this time, why?

I wanted to cry over how you unremorsefully broke my heart and how shattered you left me in your wake.

But I was unable to move and I continued to stay silent. You wanted to soften the blow with your diplomatic words of how you would always be there for me but all I could see was the irony of how you could not. You wanted to break off with me gently but all you did was twist the knife deeper into my wound and look at me indifferently as I gasped in pain.

I never had any proper closure of us. One moment we were

together and the next we were torn apart. We were suddenly strangers leading our own separate lives.

I guess what made it so hard was not losing you but the way I did. You were suddenly gone and I wasn't prepared for it. You promised me forever but turned and ran the instant things proved to be too much. You traded your promises to me for apologies and goodbyes.

Moving on from you without any closure made me question my self-worth if there was anything that I could have done differently to avoid this. I started wondering if any of it was real and if your feelings for me were true. I started to build a wall instead of relationships, believing everyone would eventually leave.

But slowly but surely, I walked out from the shadow of our past. It was difficult at first, but I slowly learned to trust and to believe that not everyone will hurt me like you did. I stopped searching for answers and realized that none of that matters anymore.

For to truly move on, I had to stop looking for closure. And that is the only closure I need.

4

We Were Only Destined To Be Ashes

Natalia Vela

Some days I forget. You. Me. *Us.* The *us* that never was. Our weaving in and out of each other's lives. The decade I pretended all you were was a friend.

Then there are days I put on an old pair of unwashed skinny jeans and find you tucked in at the bottom of my back pocket. Other times I know exactly where your memories and the fantasies we made up are, and I take them out from beneath the bed on days I don't feel anything and breathe back life into them (trying to breathe back life into myself.)

Sometimes, when I do, indifference grabs my hand and I don't know if it's towards you or if it's my depression. Other times it does bring back sensation and wrings out the numbness dripping over my entire soul and body. Sometimes it makes me write little things on paper like:

maybe it's not that
we weren't supposed to
love each other,
maybe it's just that
we were supposed to
love this way
—love in silence,
love apart,
in distance
and in flames.
maybe you and I
were made for ashes.

Sometimes I think I could hate you. Sometimes I do hate you. Sometimes I feel repulsed thinking about all the things I did I'd never do because they were for you.

Sometimes I despise even myself for ripping off all my clothes, handing you a jug of gasoline to drench over my barren body and for letting you kiss me with matchstick lips each time you had to leave.

I know you always said "I love you" like a promise you couldn't keep. But I wished what you felt would have been worth the risk. I wished whatever love was there was worth burning cities to the ground. Call me selfish, but back then I wished our happiness would have been worth someone else's pain, someone else's anger. For you, I would have left a thousand hims.

I always felt like your atoms and mine were maybe spawned from the same star. Souls bound by a cosmic chord strumming a melody only we could hear between us. Inexplicable moments when I could feel your grip on me, through the countless space and the cruel wind separating our lips. I always thought it must mean something. This feeling. The fact you told me you believed in fate – our fate. But the truth is that the moments I've felt you most you've had your hand intertwined in another's, and though I'm thinking of you today, feeling you again, it doesn't mean a thing.

We weren't from the same star. We were two different ones that came too close, and it was just all too much. We were two black holes colliding. **Neither one of us would have made it out alive but only you and I will ever know what it looked like on the inside.**

I can't have you in my life because anytime I've fallen out of love with you and see you walk into a room, hear your voice, you call me love and I'm back to filling up the gas jug. I've said it before. I don't want to burn. Not for you. *Not anymore.* Next time I think I'll keep you in my back pocket until you burn a hole. Until the debris spills. After all, all we ever were destined to be was ashes.

5

I Guess They Name Hurricanes After People For A Reason

Casandra Nguyen

I always have fancied the thought of storms, in my own twisted way. There's just something about the way the sky apologizes with a rainbow after a storm that puts me at ease. *You can't have sunshine without a little rain, right?*

All of this appeared to be true until you came along. Like a hurricane, you were the most violent storm I have ever experienced. You didn't come with a storm warning so I didn't have time to evacuate or board up my windows.

I'm still dealing with the aftermath.

I should've left when I discovered the magnitude of the storm you'd bring. I ignored my head and trusted with all my heart that you wouldn't destroy a home you helped build. I thought I was ready to face the whirlwind—*I had no idea.*

It wasn't supposed to be like this. You were supposed to kiss my skin like the sun in July and warm my insides like a cappuccino in December. I only had a shitty umbrella and rain boots but realistically, I needed a storm shelter. No one saw this coming—*I didn't see this coming.*

We were supposed to be just friends. Storms are supposed to bring peace but instead, this one brought chaos. I was supposed to be watching the rain crash into my window but instead, I was caught right in the eye of the storm.

The only way out of the storm was to go through it and that's exactly what I did.

You crashed into the walls that I spent years building around my soul and exposed my weak structure for all to see. When the damage was done, little pieces of me remained. You flooded the streets and took pieces of me wherever you went and left them to rot. Your words crashed into me but no one heard because you said them in solitude; like a fallen tree in a forest. It's been a while since you last caused destruction.

After all, most hurricanes form but never make it out of the ocean.

The pain during the storm was bad but the agony after is worse. I see the wreckage in everything you tampered with. The casualty count is still rising. My hope for our future is dead, along with the belief that someone can love you without hurting you.

I'm still rebuilding my home but this time I won't use false hope as the glue to hold it all together.

Homes made out of people will never survive unharmed.

As for you, you're off the coast now. But I'm sure you'll be back when the waters get warm again. In typical fashion, you'll unexpectedly decide to come crashing in when you become yesterday's news.

After all, hurricanes are named after people like you for a reason.

6

No One Wants To Love A Sad Girl

Shrina Dutta

No one wants to love a sad girl. She is neither the daisies nor the roses. She doesn't find spring at her feet. She is the melancholic thoughts with an anxious mind. She finds comfort in wearing turtlenecks to cover her face when she cries. She is the one to be late for dates because she has been racing back and forth in her apartment deciding whether or not to go. She cannot bring life to the room with her rings of laughter because she is busy staring at something unknown. You cannot take pride over her like a shiny penny you have collected because she always looks so exhausted.

No one wants to love a sad girl because she is a forever battle you are afraid you will be forced to fight. She makes problems out of nothing and nothing out of everything. She is not spontaneous. She is not the one to sit by the bonfire humming a sweet tune with hair all over her face that you gently tuck behind her ears. Instead, you have to hold her hair back tight with her face over the toilet seat vomiting all over.

No one wants to love a sad girl because she is not easy. She has a baggage. She is not that girl on TV you wish you have. No day is the same. No one knows what the next moment will bring in. She is not the one to look perfect in your T-shirt and Calvins with the perfect pair of lips sipping a smoothie through a straw. She is not your manic-pixie dream girl. She does not care for the thousand bucks spent on makeup or the wasted gym membership.

No one wants to love a sad girl because when you first saw her she did not look sad. She had well, a strong face and a sharp tongue. And, you enjoyed it. You seemed to like that edge but not so much when she started telling her story and you started seeing her phases. You panicked. You do not want that. You do not want to be that person who could not make her happy even though you were the one and every reason who made her try to be happy. You wanted the same version of every story with a side of extra pepper. And so you don't. And it's okay because she deserves the mountain while you are just a pebble of the ocean.

What Does She Have That I Didn't?

Nicole Tarkoff

I sometimes wonder what she has that I didn't.

Does she lead a more interesting life? Drive a cooler car and make a larger salary. Does she dress in name-brand clothing and wear shinier jewelry? Lather her lips in designer gloss and powder her face with a shade of rosier blush. Does she care about all the things I never did?

Does she speak with words that I'm not smart enough to understand? Graduate from a fancier college with a fancier degree. Does she read books about topics that I never found interesting? Does she initiate the kinds of conversations I never would?

Does she have curves in all the places that I don't? Have poutier lips and plumper cheeks. Does she have a tinier nose and more sculpted brow? Does her appearance look all the ways mine never did?

Does she laugh at all of your jokes? Agree with all of your opinions. Never start meaningless arguments that have no end. Does she ever do *anything* wrong? Does she think you're always right?

Does she cater to your every need? Worry about your happiness more than she does her own. Does she ever complain about her terrible day or the stress she has at work? Ever just feel sad for no apparent reason and have no idea why. Does she pretend to always be okay? Hide her negative feelings so well that you have yet to find them. Does she have any negative feelings at all? Is she *just enough* in every way that I was *too much*? Is she simple in every way that I was complicated?

Does she give you a kind of love I never did? Display her affection so publicly that everyone knows you belong to her and she belongs to you. Does she say 'I love you,' 10 times each day? Text it to you while you're at work and out with friends. Does she never crave alone time or just need to get away? Is she completely infatuated with you every hour of every day? Does she ever make you doubt the love she has for you in every way that I did?

I had everything that made you leave. What does she have that finally made you stay? Is she everything I'm not? Everything I'll never be? These are the questions I asked myself after you left me, the questions I asked myself when I learned you promised to never do the same to her.

These are the questions that don't matter.

She and I are very different people, and even if she was *exactly* like me, you chose her, not me. You continue to choose her. When I asked myself these questions, when I made these extravagantly damaging comparisons, I never realized that they were only postponing the time when I'd find the person who chooses me.

Questioning what she has that I don't slows that entire process. It prevents me from accepting everything I am, everything I have, and everything I don't, every flaw that I'll never be able to get rid of, and every beautiful imperfection that I continuously struggle to appreciate. Constantly comparing myself to her, convinces me that she's more deserving of the love I should be giving to myself.

She is not me. She is not the person I was when I was with you, and she will never be the person I strive to become. I accepted that, and sooner or later I found him, the person who loves me, the person who *chooses* to love me. **He is everything you never were.**

8

On Letting People And Things Go

Becca Martin

I woke up from a text from one of my coworkers this morning about an article I wrote yesterday. The article was about how friendships ending can also break your heart. I jokingly texted her back about how I am very good at letting people go.

Then I thought nothing of it as I continued to lay in bed for about 20 minutes like I do every morning, just scrolling through all my social media apps.

Once it hits around 7:45 I get up and head to the kitchen to make my morning coffee. I grab the mug I always use out of the cabinet and stick it under the Keurig. I make my two eggs and Ezekiel toast like I do every morning. I call Disney about a ticket I had that was from 1998 to see if it was still valid—it wasn't, but the one from 2009 was. I eat breakfast at my kitchen bar and then come into the office as soon as I finish eating. I don't even put my dirty dishes away, not until lunchtime, anyway.

Then it hit me as I took my last sip of coffee and put the mug down that's completely faded and barely readable that I do have a hard time letting things go. Not only people but also things.

I like things that are worn and torn. My favorite sweatshirt is one of my dad's old police sweatshirts. The sleeves are ripped, it looks like something that should have been thrown away 20 years ago, but it's my favorite. I have no problem wearing it out in public. I don't want to throw it away, so I keep it.

I always fought with my mom over getting new shoes, which is kind of ridiculous. She always told me I needed a new pair, but I never wanted to let the old pair go. She'd even sometimes come home with a new pair of shoes (of the exact same pair I had) so she could throw the old pair out. It's kind of funny actually (and slightly pathetic) how attached to things I get.

I don't like change unless it's me changing. I was talking to another one of my coworkers about this when I was staying with her in NYC. We joked about how we hate change unless we are the ones who change. Which is completely selfish, but it's true. I want to be able to go far away and change and love and learn, but when I go back home I want everything to be exactly the same. I want to go back to my house, I want my roommates to be there, I want all my friends to be there, I want everything to be the same, but nothing is. And I have a hard time accepting that. I have a hard time accepting how fast things can change.

I have a hard time letting go of the things I love.

I can't even read my coffee mug anymore, but I know it said: "there's always room for one more dog" only because I bought it as a way to convince my mom we should get another dog. She didn't fall for it, but it was worth a shot.

And that leads me back to friendships, again. I've been single for about 6 years, there's been the "we're just talking" things in there many times, but no one I would consider a total heartbreak. Well, maybe there's one. Whatever. My friends have been my life. They're the ones I call when I get lonely, the ones I cry to when I'm sad, the ones I run all my life decisions through because they're all I've got.

My friends understand me more than I understand myself I like to believe. They're the best people I know. I'm that friend who randomly texts my friends all the time. I try to talk to as many of them as possible just so they don't forget about me. They're all out in the world moving forward with their lives in new cities with new friends making new memories, and I'm not. Not right now, anyway.

I don't want them to move on without me and I know how selfish that is but I feel like I'll be forgotten about and no one wants to feel forgotten about. I guess it's because it happens, it's happened to me plenty of times before.

It happened in high school with my best friend when I left for college. He forgot about me, I left our hometown and he stayed, both of our lives went on, just without each other. It happened with one of my best friends in college, we did everything together until he moved and ever since then he has barely spoken to me. Of course, it happened a third time with my other best friend in college. I moved to Australia, he got a girlfriend and he just stopped talking to me one day. It hurt, those times all hurt and sometimes (most of the time) they still do.

People forget about you when you're no longer together and that's what I try so desperately to avoid.

I think I've been okay with being single for so long because I cling to my guy friends, I get all my emotional male needs from them and that's why I've been okay with being on my own. I understand my girl friends, I get them and they get me. But you don't get the same amount of satisfaction from your girl friends as you do from guy friends. At least I don't.

So I try, which is pathetic. I still reach out to all of them from time to time, most of the time my messages go unanswered, but I tell myself it's worth a shot because I just can't let go. I don't give up on people. I'm really bad at giving up.

I can't let go of people and I can't let go of things. I'm not good at moving on and letting go. I'm not good at just moving forward with my life because I miss the past too much. I'm convinced nothing will ever be as good as it once was, and so far things have always gotten better. But what happens when things stop getting better? What happens when I wake up one morning and realize I'm completely alone, when I don't have the people I once had in my life, when all my friendships and relationships fail?

What do I do then?

I always talk about moving forward, but I'm terrified of it and I think that's why I just keep pushing myself. Everyone around me is moving on and I'm still hanging on to dear life over relationships that should have been over years ago and items that the Salvation Army would turn down. But to me they mean something, to me they reflect my past and I don't think I'm ready to let them go still.

I hang on because I'm always the one who cares more, the one who's more invested and I hate to see the things I care about fall apart. I always wondered why this was, but now I'm realizing that I've always been like this. I was like this when I refused to get new shoes, I was like this when I refused to give ratty old clothes away, but had no problem throwing a shirt with a tag on it to the Salvation Army pile. **And as I drink out of my old faded coffee mug I realized that I hold on so close to people because I want someone to hold on to me that way, but no one does *and no one ever has.***

9

What To Do When You're Convinced You'll Never Find Love Again

Ari Eastman

Breathe.

Seriously, just breathe.

Maybe put on that Michelle Branch "Breathe" to really drive the message home.

Text your best friend something ridiculously dramatic like, "I am 100% going to die alone." Joke about replacing your heart with a block of ice. Look up cabins in the middle of nowhere and research how to get licensed as a dog sanctuary.

Think about the last time your heart flipped when someone touched your knee. Think about how it felt to look at another person and see forever reflected back in their eyes. Think about the longing. The aching. The dizziness. Think about the electricity before that first kiss. Think about how high it made you. How drunk off nothingness. Think about their mouth and involuntarily shiver.

Text your best friend again. "Fuck this shit."

Google inspirational quotes. Roll your eyes at all of them.

Keep listening to Michelle Branch. She was your JAM back in the day. Watch all of the lyrics come back to you. Wonder if this means you never forget anything. Wonder if this means you hang on even when you're not meaning to.

Mindlessly swipe on dating apps. No. No. No.

Text someone you used to love.

Study your reflection in the mirror. Feel bitter. Feel bitter that this person looking back is so closed off. This person doesn't even want to fall in love anymore.

Splash water on your face. Yes, you're every character in every movie ever. Everything you do has been done before. This feeling, this questioning. It's not original.

You are not the first person to be lonely. You are not the first person to be convinced love isn't going to be on the menu again.

Somehow find comfort in it. Find comfort in the universality of it all. In the sameness. In the people who've cried the same tears you have. In the people who've stubbornly decided they're done. In the people who weren't done. In the love that shows back up unexpectedly. In the love that surprises. In the love that knocks when you stop fussing about when it's coming.

Just breathe.

Go ahead and turn Michelle Branch all the way up.

10

Maybe One Day I Won't Miss You

Marisa Donnelly

Maybe one day I won't look at old pictures of us and throw myself back in time, feeling your hands on my skin, remembering the curve of your smile or the way you'd look into my eyes and I swear, everything else around me would blur out of focus.

Maybe one day I won't have to pick up the phone to call you, hear your voice distorted by phone lines and static, interrupted by spotty service, muffled as you start drifting into sleep.

Maybe one day I won't have to close my eyes and imagine your kiss on my cheek, won't have to roll over in my big, empty bed and pretend the fortress I've made of pillows is your body, soft and warm and strong next to mine.

Maybe one day I won't have this ache, dull and numbing in the center of my chest, reminding me of what I had, of what I've lost.

Maybe one day I won't have to pretend I'm fine here, pushing through my days, lying to myself about where you are and what you're doing. Acting as if I don't think of you, even though I can't get you out of my head.

Maybe one day it won't have to be like this, miles and unspoken words between us, promises that we tried so desperately to keep but fell flat in our mouths like stale soda. Emptiness filling us instead.

Maybe one day I won't have to wish, won't have to feign indifference, won't have to be reminded of you in every step, every song, every single day.

Maybe one day I won't have to miss you. Because you'll be here.

Because we'll stop these games we play with one another's hearts. Because we'll finally grow up and tell one another how we feel. Because we'll decide that distance cannot, will not have power over who we are and could become.

Because we'll believe in love far more than we fall victim to fear.

And then we'll step forward in faith. We'll reach for one another's hands. We'll stop letting the past dictate our future, or our hesitancy allow us to miss out on a possibility. We'll quit talking ourselves out of a potential romance. We'll push the negative thoughts from our mind and focus on the good.

We'll quit trying to control love, plan love, analyze love and let it happen. Let our hearts feel, our minds get dizzy, our bodies touch, our spirits align, and our longing finally cease.

Maybe one day we won't have all these hypotheticals, these 'maybes' these ideas that never fall to fruition. Maybe one day we'll be confident enough to trust ourselves, to trust one another, to trust that love isn't just a fading aspect of this generation, but something real.

Maybe one day we won't have to feel so separated, so distant, so scared because we'll be here. In the present. In one another's arms.

Maybe one day I won't have to miss you.
Because you'll be mine.

11

This Is How You Become 'The One That Got Away'

Brynn Taylor

Quickly after my last relationship ended, there was an uncontrollable amount of grief and self-reflection. Instead of accepting that it was over, I began to try to put the pieces back together.

When we met, I pictured every moment of our future together. As we got closer, I began to define my self-worth as his girlfriend, so when it ended, I lost sight of the person I thought I would become. I lost sight of "me," and just wondered what life would be like without "us."

After the breakup, I wasted no time thinking about all the moments that were wonderful and thinking about how hard each upcoming moment would be without him beside me.

In these moments, the grief seemed uncontrollable. In these

moments, were the times that I started to think, ***This might be the one that gets away.***

But I did everything in my power to stop it, despite all the warning signals.

If he's such a horrible person, why do I still want him here now?

If things were so bad, then how come I picture these moments with him that could be so good?

Why do I believe so immensely, that if I had done everything right, that he would still be with me?

For me, when you start to blame yourself, that's when someone becomes the one that got away. That's when you think, *I haven't done enough, and if things were different, they would still be here.*

Some people will experience this sort of grief all at once, while others will shut down because they don't want to reflect or grieve. They just ignore the pain for as long as they can, coming up with excuses or ways to blame everything else but themselves.

When people aren't ready to face the music, they choose to overlook their mistakes. They choose to put the blame elsewhere. They decide that some other contributing factor, like timing, will eventually be better and that a loss has nothing to do with them.

They figure that next time, things will just miraculously be different.

And yes, timing is everything, but that is because there will eventually be a time when two people who are ready meet, and they will be both be open to working on their problems.

I always believed the timing was off when I noticed someone in the relationship had so much more to learn, myself included, but I refused to learn anyway. I figured that the timing must've been off because that person, at that time, was not ready to put in the work, so it couldn't have been right.

For me, letting "the one" get away because of timing was never a viable option. For me, the pain hits too hard and too fast. Instead, I look for every possible explanation I can find, seeking what went wrong and working to fix it.

I begin to try to learn from my mistakes. Although remembering them is rarely enjoyable, I want to learn right away, so I choose to acknowledge them.

I want to make sure I never look back and say, "that was the one that got away."

As miserable as it may seem, after someone experiences heartbreak, they can start to look for the mistakes that brought them to that point and learn how to be a better partner.

While searching for answers as to why we lost a lover, there is a powerful impact on our sense of self. I believe that by taking that learning experience, we become more ready to try again.

I believe that if you can grow, you'll find someone who can grow with you, and you'll never need to look back and wonder why things didn't work out.

Reflections can be crippling, so some people fear them. But they are also rehabilitating. Accepting responsibility gives us the power to overcome any mistakes that we make. It is not letting our mistakes define us, but rather having them help us grow.

Being in a relationship involves accepting responsibility for our actions, and how they affect another person. If someone is ready to be in one, they don't let small mistakes build up until one person feels the weight of the world on their shoulders; the weight is distributed equally.

So when do you become the one that got away? When do past loves look back and say, that was a great girl, how did I let her go? How did I let all these things get in the way of our relationship?

I have seen it happen, and yet I can't fathom why anyone could say that when they were the one who ended things.

How does anyone live their life saying there was a "one that got away," without ever making a single attempt at figuring out what they could have done to stop it? When you gave so many chances that they didn't deserve, and they didn't take a single one of them?

Why am I the one that got away, when he was the one that didn't try?

Why was I the one taking the blame for so long, and him the one thinking everything was all my fault?

I sat there thinking that he was the one that got away for so long when I was always meant to be the one that got away.

When I took the time to learn to define myself and my mistakes with that person, I could also define myself without them. And one day he will be sitting scratching his head, thinking maybe the timing didn't work, when in reality, it was just him that didn't put in the work.

In these moments, the grief becomes controllable. We begin to become rehabilitated, and the strength re-enters our bodies.

We learn that by getting through the pain, we can get through anything.

I was always the one with the strong heart, who was designed to learn from my mistakes and to grow into an even greater person. I was never looking for something to blame. I was always accepting responsibility.

Sometimes the timing IS off, because the one you want to be the great person for, made the choice to leave. But you will always be the one who will stay.

There are certain girls in this world who are made up to be powerful partners. Ones that don't wait until it's too late to see what they have right in front of them.

Ones who, even in dark times, think about what they could have done wrong, and can reevaluate themselves and learn to do things right.

And if someone won't accept that, then you can do right by someone else.

If someone doesn't want to work on things with you, you can work on your mistakes without them.

You will move on. You will find someone better. **Because you were always better.**

You are only the one that got away because they *let* you.

12

Tell Her You Love Her

Lacey Ramburger

Tell her you love her, that you have never loved anyone else the way you love her.

Then remember the way you loved me.

And the way you still love me, even now.

The way you pretend not to in the day to day, but you still see me everywhere-our memories have painted your eyes, and you still see me even when I'm nowhere to be found. The way that at night when you're alone, my voice still bounces around in the midst of all the other thoughts you have- a steady bass drum that doesn't demand attention, but continuously repeats, refusing to let you forget.

Pretend like you don't think about my eyes; the way they looked at you like you were the only person in the room, the way I could tune out everything else besides us, even when your eyes kept wandering. Pretend like you've forgotten the sound of my laughter; remember how I was completely unafraid to look silly or foolish around you, despite how often you managed to make me feel that way. Remember the way I held your hand, no matter how often you decided to pull it away.

Remember how at one time, I spent all of my energy and effort trying to make you understand the extent of my feelings, and how you turned away and claimed ignorance, pretending you didn't notice.

Remember how you listened to all the voices in your head saying to walk away, telling you there were other options- better ones. Remember how you tried to fill the void I left with dozens of things, and how by the time you figured out that nothing came close, I was gone.

Because it is true that I tend to stay, I am loyal, and I will fight harder than anyone to make something work. Yet once I've walked away, there is no going back.

You set me free hoping you would get freedom yourself. You set me free not knowing or caring how it might affect me because you assumed you'd be happier. Until it turned out that I was the one who was finally free. I was the one who ended up happy, to both of our surprise. It was you who would try to get rises out of me, try to convince me to come back, try to say you made a mistake and tell me over and over how you had changed.

But it didn't matter. Because once the feelings left, I had no desire to return.

And now, you try to move on. You talk to pretty faces and you tell them they are your favorite. You develop feelings for one and you try to live your life.

You tell her you love her and that you've never loved anyone else the way you loved her.

Of course you haven't. But does she know you will never love anyone else the way you loved me?

Does she know the way you love her, will always be a little less?

13

University Lovers

David Lorenzo

"Hey my lecture ends in 15, let's get lunch?"

Texts like this could be exchanged frequently between me and you. We go to a school with over 20,000 people, but I would be fine if it was just us two. You and I should be university lovers; there's so much we could do.

Like going to basketball games to join the crowd that's wearing all gold. Or get drunk together at the college bars, at least until that gets old. We could go to the library, to the floors where no one goes. I kiss you once, you kiss me twice; no one has to know.

University lovers you and I should be, but we don't hang out and we don't really talk. So I guess we'll have to see. You send me a Snap, I send you one back. That might be the best we can do. But if we were university lovers, I'd call you up to see if you could come through.

Our schedules don't match, so there goes that. It's so hard to coordinate plans. I want you and you want him; this is completely out of my hands. She texts me and he texts you, that's how this story ends. University lovers, I know it won't happen.

But at least I can pretend.

14

Why I'll Always Love You More Than Anyone Else

Heidi Priebe

I'll always love you most because discovering you wasn't just discovering you—it wasn't learning your favorite bands and meeting your parents and tracing my fingers through the valleys of your skin. Discovering you was discovering love. It was discovering redemption. It was discovering Saturday mornings waking up in bed beside somebody else and not wanting to gather up my clothing and sneak out. It was discovering letting someone see me—all my failures and my fuck-ups and my raw, uncomfortable honesties and realizing that they could love me anyway. It was seeing someone else's ugliness and insecurity and pain and realizing that I could love them anyway, too. That I could stare down the murkiest, most unsavory realities of somebody's character and want to choose them all the more because of them. I will always love you more than anybody else because I saw the worst in you and you saw the worst in me and we lived in those ugly, unsavory houses our mistakes made. We were residents of them, together. We survived them. And they still feel like the only honest truth. I'll always love you more than anyone else because everyone else is just a blueprint. Just a skeleton, a ghost of what we once unearthed and discovering them isn't discovering anything new. Every other body is only a body. Every other mind is just a system of synapses and neurons, firing in time alongside mine. I will always love you the most because when you grow up in a room that you're sure is sealed shut, the second window you discover is just a window. Just a nice view, no matter which direction it gazes out on. I will always love you most because you were the first goddamned window. Because loving you broke through a wall that I didn't realize could be punctured. Because loving you made me realize we are not meant to stay sealed shut in the room with all our pains and mistakes. Because you were the first breath of fresh air. Air I never expected to breathe. And after that first hit of oxygen, nothing ever tastes quite as sweet again.

15

How To Properly Destroy Yourself

Eric Corey

First, go to community college. Here, you will pick up smoking cigarettes. Begin to resent your friends from high school because of the prestige and fun that comes with living hours away. Eventually, they'll grow tired of your side-remarks and backhanded compliments. You will think you hit rock bottom when you go on a midnight drive with no one but the family dog to keep you company; you aren't there yet.

Go away to university. Pick a liberal arts major, and live with someone who drinks. Pick up drinking from them, socially at first. Only on weekends. Only at parties. Turn twenty-one and realize the magic of Thirsty Thursdays. It's ok because you always drink with people.

Join a co-ed club and fall desperately in love with the president. Be there for her, for once in your life not because you think of women as vending machines, but because you actually mean it when you say, *"I'd rather you be happy with someone else."* Convince yourself that she isn't happy with someone else (this will be easy because you'd accept any excuse to be with her).

Start an affair, and hide it from everyone close to you. Start drinking every day. Enter therapy at age 22, get drunk and call that therapist. Tell her she won't tell you anything you don't know, and never see her again.

Here, you will realize that you spend more money at the bars than you do on your bills. Justify it, knowing that every college kid drinks and every college kid is poor. End your affair, and feel empty. It's easy to convince yourself that you're unfixable and that people would be better off; once you do this, you can enter your final stage of destruction. The countdown has begun.

Jump into a relationship. Sleep with this new person in your ex-lovers bed, and laugh it off. Ignore every attempt by your friends to sit you down and talk to you about your behavior. Take this new girlfriend, a fine person who never did anything wrong to you, and break up with her. Tell her it's because you still have feelings for the former girlfriend. She will, of course, tell you to drink yourself to death.

Convince yourself she's right, and the rest comes easy.

16

This Is How You Heal From Him

Claire Windsor

You heal from him by deciding to wake up every morning. Even if, for a while, you don't even make it out of bed. But by still waking up, even though he's not beside you, you've already made the choice to not let him keep you down. By still waking up, and having the bravery to face what could be ahead of you, you're choosing yourself instead of him.

You heal from him in moments, in small things, in little firsts. Like, the first time you have dinner that isn't just a wine bottle and sobs. The first time you go out for coffee and his name doesn't pass your lips. The first time you smile at someone new and don't feel regret or guilt. The first time you sleep soundly and without nightmares. The first time you go most of a day without missing him.

You heal from him by acknowledging he hurt you in the first place. You look at the moments where he made you feel small, or unheard, or cracked, or unloved. You dissect them, break them open, examine each little bit and fiber and molecule of why things were maybe not what they seemed. You look at them, and you realize and say out loud, *He wasn't as perfect as I thought.*

You heal from him by acknowledging that you weren't perfect either. That you are also flawed, and difficult, and can be less than enough. You recognize your own shortcomings and your own cracks that lead you to this place. And after putting yourself under a microscope for examination, you decide to be better. For others, yes. But mostly for yourself.

You heal from him by actively choosing to let him go. By refusing to linger, to obsess, to fester after you've looked at him and yourself and what was. You don't keep picking at the wound; you leave it alone. You don't keep nagging at the hurt; you let it be. You say enough is enough, and you turn your back and you let things go.

You heal from him by giving yourself time. By accepting that healing isn't a race, and that there's not a set course to follow. By allowing yourself to grieve and to have ups and downs and good days and bad days. By soothing yourself for the days when you aren't as strong, and cheering for yourself on the days when you are. But by remembering that there's no one size fits all guide to healing, and your roadmap is yours and yours alone.

You heal from him by forgiving. Not forgetting, but saying that it's okay. But that you're okay. And furthermore, that you know you'll *be* okay.

You heal from him by remembering you loved him. By remembering the things about him that were enough, and were more than enough. By remembering the promises you made and the smiles that he caused. By remembering that the part of you that loved him would be disappointed in you both for hurting each other, yes, but it would also be disappointed to see you refuse to be the versions of yourselves that are happy. That are free. That are healed.

When I Said 'Hi', I Meant 'I Love You'

Amanda Tarlton

Hi.

That's the text I sent you, that's always the text I send you. The one I send when I haven't heard from you in a few days or when I'm a little too drunk on Friday night or when I'm laying in bed alone.

It's the text that's supposed to sound casual like I don't care if you respond or not, like I'm the chill laid-back girl every guy falls for in the movies.

But I don't want to say hi.

I want to say I miss you.

That I miss how you hugged me, how I fit so perfectly underneath your arm. I miss how you're the only one who still called me by my nickname, how you had that one crooked dimple when you smiled. I even miss how we always had to listen to that boring talk radio in your Jeep and how you could fall asleep in the middle of a conversation.

I want to say come over.

That I'd do anything for you to walk through my door right now, anything to have another night curled up beside you. That I don't sleep anymore, my mascara-stained pillow proof of long nights remembering what we once had, what we will never have again. That waking up without you on Saturday mornings hurts so much I can barely get out of bed.

I want to say you're the only thing I think about.

That you're the only one I want to kiss, the only one I want to hold me when I'm sad, the only one I want to meet me at the end of the aisle. That some days I sit in my office staring at the computer screen and wonder if you're thinking of me, too. If you missed another deadline because you can't focus on anything else.

I want to say I've never felt so lonely.

That I make excuses to go to your favorite bar hoping to run into you. That when I go on dates with other men, I wish it was you there instead of sitting across the table. That no one else can fill the space you left in my heart, no one else makes me feel as beautiful, as loved or as special as you did.

I want to say she isn't right for you.

That she may be prettier and more successful and mature than me but she wouldn't put your life in front of her own. That she doesn't know you the way I do, doesn't know how you secretly love the Bachelor or how you need your alone time when you're mad. That she is a good "for now" but I could be a good "forever".

Most of all, I want to say I still love you.

That I will always love you, no matter how much time has passed or how many people tell me to move on. That you will always have my heart, even if I no longer have yours. That I will always be there for you, whether I'm 24 or 84 or even 104.

So every time the clock says 11:11, I'll keep wishing. Wishing you'll come back, wishing for one more chance, wishing to hear you whisper those three words again.

And until then, until I can say I love you, I'll just send you that text.

Hi.

18

Five Crucial Things To Remember When They Do Not Love You Back

Kai Masa

i. hold on. hold on but know when to unclench your fists to gently set things free. hold on but know when to let go. hold on but let go when you have to. it doesn't mean you love them any less when you do.

ii. there may be days when this world reminds you of all that you are not; of all that you couldn't be. it may have made you feel as if you aren't enough but please be patient with yourself. there is a universe of possibilities inside of you and you only ever need the courage to dive into them.

iii. let yourself heal. plant daydreams in the cracks on your heart. stitch the gaping spaces in your chest with tears if you have to. let your heart heal the way it knows how. darling, you could only be better if you allow yourself to be.

iv. your heart is more than just someone else's home. it is yours too. your heart is your home and it will always be.

v. learn to love yourself on your dark days. learn to love yourself when you can't seem to love any part of you when your heart is too heavy with darkness and sadness is all that has kept you company. learn to love yourself and learn to let others love you.

19

A Thank You Letter To All The People Who Let Me Down

Rania Naim

At first, I was hurt. I was angry. I was bitter but then I became grateful because when you let me down, you answered every question I had—questions I never thought would be answered.

Thank you for making me cry, the tears washed away the mist that stopped me from seeing your true colors all these years but now I see things more clearly. The tears made me realize that I was blinded by your vision. I believed everything you told me about myself and I avoided mirrors because all I saw were the imperfections you pointed out, the flaws you would always remind me of and the person you told me I was. So thank you for the tears, I can now see the good things you never magnified, the positive qualities that you kept suppressing so you can shine, and now I don't avoid mirrors. **Now I look at myself** with pride because I see the person I could become. The person you told me I could never be.

Thank you for taking your love away from me. Thank you for not telling me things I needed to hear to love myself. Thank you for not showering me with the love and support I needed to thrive. Thank you for constantly reminding me that I'll never find love in your arms because you forced to fight for another kind of love. You forced me to find a *better* kind of love. You forced to love myself without your help and **you forced me to look for the kind of love you never had, the kind of love you never knew.** You made me realize that all you knew was a hostile kind of love. The kind of love that hurts and offends people. The kind of love that keeps score. The kind of love that turns into a war of who cares less, who's always wrong and who can lose faster. **Thank you for showing what kind of love I really don't need in my life.**

Thank you for letting me down and abandoning me. You forced me to *upgrade.* You forced me to find myself. Your forced me to find better and more loving people and you forced me to find a better life. A life where I don't have to be condemned for being human, making mistakes, learning or growing up. A life where I can be myself and still feel *safe.* **A life where speaking up doesn't cost you an arm and a leg. A life where love is freely given without any tears, bruises or injuries.**

20

For Seven Minutes My Heart Stops, And I See You

Bianca Sparacino

After the heart stops there are seven minutes of brain activity left. Seven minutes, four hundred twenty seconds, where the brain plays back movie memories of what shaped it—like a homage to the organ, like a final goodbye to the restless dreamers that lived by it and to the unwavering capacity by which they loved through it.

During the first minute, I saw you. I saw you as if it were the first time, and my god you were perfect. I saw the bad chat, the coy smiles, the terrible dance moves and the genuine laughter. I saw you pick me up and take me into your arms, I saw you lean in for our first kiss. I saw me beaming on my way home, spell bound thinking, "This is something big. This is going to ruin me."

Minute two and three. I saw the flicker of our flame. I saw the way your bones played with the moonlight, the way your back looked against the night sky as we slept under the canopy of our favorite city. I saw the letters you wrote me, scrawled in graphite along the surface of my skin. I saw the man you were trying to become, the intelligently awe-inspiring man you were working towards. I saw the clock, as we counted down the days, gripping tighter and tighter within our false reality until I saw the goodbye.

Minute four. I saw the hurt. I saw it riddled across your face like a cold sweat. I saw the last embrace and the heaviness that came with having to let go. I saw the confusion, the need to simply make sense of what we had shared, of what we didn't want to give up on. I saw the scramble within both of our souls, the human parts of us trying to make up the miles, trying to fit the world into a shoe box so we could fill the void. I saw the suffering.

Minute five and six. I saw the girl who found you at the right time. I saw how you kissed her with my warmth on your mouth; how you tried to place yourself into her open arms like a jagged puzzle piece that simply did not fit. I saw my hope for you during that time; the impatient and genuine hope that you would be cured of this memory, that you would be able to sleep beside the bones of another without dreaming of a ghost.

But before I knew it, I met minute seven, and despite all of the hurt, all of the feeling, all of the unanswered questions—I saw the communion of hues, the colours of every sunset I had ever witnessed, come together to build the contours of your face. I saw the purples of your under eyes, I saw the whites of your teeth. I saw the pinks of your lips and the reds that made up the flush in your cheek. I saw the man who shaped me, the man who dug my heart up like dinosaur bones. I saw you whisper goodbye, and it was then, only then, in the beauty of your night sky, that I finally moved on.

21

Four Sentences On How It Ended

Katie Mather

I don't think I'd ever described myself as LOUD and I asked Kendra what she thought and she told me that I'm only loud when I'm trying to say something I think is important (additionally, but unrelated: also when I'm drunk and/or heated)—and the only reason why I was asking her this in the first place is because towards The End I was entirely silent, and I can't tell if that's a fault of my overall character or telling of how numb I was to everything that was happening.

Growing up, I had trouble saying goodbye to things and places and especially people, and sometimes I would have to collect myself and pause and really force the images of these things and places and people I was saying goodbye to into my memory in order to make the whole experience tolerable—*I am terrified of forgetting things and my mind is stuffed with goodbyes and thoughts of "this might be the last time I see this"*—but I didn't realize that we were saying goodbye and I didn't consider that this might be the last time I see you, so I didn't take down any notes or imprint any images and I stayed entirely quiet.

I feel like I should've been LOUDER because I definitely had a lot of things to say that I think are important—or at least, as I was leaving, I should've taken a couple mental images to replay over and over in my head until I feel dizzy and sick with nostalgia and regret—but instead I stayed silent and didn't look at anything in particular and don't even remember enough basic details to accurately play what happened over and over.

And that's what I've always been worried might happen and I'm sad it happened with you.

22

Chaos Magic

Chrissy Stockton

My friend flies to LA for the purpose of going to a party in the hills he feels like going to. He says you have to light money on fire and watch it burn. You have to tell the universe "these are the motherfucking rules."

I go to Chicago and I eat everything I want to eat. I consume crab for breakfast two days in a row. My friend and I pick at a plate of jumbo shrimp arranged on a bed of ice (*soigné*) and share a fillet and venison and pork belly. I go back to my hotel and pay $20 for a small dish of ice cream to be delivered to my room.

I set the bowl on the window and look at the skyline and read a book about loneliness. The writer says that loneliness isn't a topic even social scientists are comfortable talking about because it's still so taboo to be lonely. She says the only people who really talk about loneliness are songwriters.

I don't know if I feel lonely sitting on that windowsill in Chicago even though I am alone. I feel the way I always do, I guess. I feel understood by the book the way people in books and people who write books have always made me feel understood. Before I knew the phrase 'irl' I knew that irl was never going to be the place I felt most at home, which is a lonely thing to know from a young age, maybe.

The world is susceptible to chaos magic, my friend says, you have to set the rules. The rule I make is that I'm not afraid of scarcity anymore. By taking this trip I am demonstrating the way I permit the world to work: *there is enough, there is a way to feel like enough.*

The reason you don't talk about a taboo is because you are afraid to lose something—the respect or admiration or affection of a person or a group of people or the world at large. The abundance I am insisting into existence is that this must not need to be true, that perhaps we are all waiting for someone else to be the first to say the terrible thing so that we can confess, too. A chorus of people saying "I'm lonely" slay the dragon just by speaking its name.

The rules are that we have to say the words. We have to say "I'm lonely" or "I'm afraid". The rules are we have to be brave enough to name each feeling as if you are simply noting a change in weather. The rules are that as soon as you do this, it is so.

23

What To Do When You Realize They've Moved On For Good

Kendra Syrdal

Draw a bath at 7:14 PM and commit yourself to staying in and feeling sorry for yourself. Forget to pay attention to the temperature and end up dunking yourself into something near boiling. Ignore it when your skin starts screaming at you. Hope that the version of you that emerges is somehow detoxified. Lighter. *Better.* That whatever you will exist in one, two, three hours won't be hung up on the fact that they're not hung up on you at all. Spill wine on yourself and watch it run down your chest into the water. Remember that everything can be cleansed, even you. Think about what it was like to be heartbroken, and in turn, what it was like to break their heart. Wonder, admittedly sadistically, how long it took for them to decide they were over you. Try to picture in your mind how they described you to other people. Imagine all the adjectives they put next to your name over the years. Close your eyes and try to remember what your name sounded like when they said it, just for a second. Try to pinpoint the emotion you're feeling because as much as you'd like to put Lorde on repeat and be heartbroken, be devastated, it's not that simple. It's not really sad, it's not really anything. It just sort of…*is*. Sit in bed and watch the hours pass, only illuminated by the glow of a computer screen. Try to write something, make something, become something that *matters*. Realize how sobering it is to come to terms with the fact that you don't matter to them anymore. That promises aren't forever. That someone's world will turn without you in it. That you have to swallow whatever narcissistic pride somehow deemed yourself, 'The One That Got Away' and realizes, you're not a 'one' at all. Read the entire Wikipedia article about the multiple universe theory and try to picture one where you ended up with them. But realize that as much as you're obsessing, you can't picture it. That you don't remember what it sounded like when they said your name. That you're not their one, and that they're not yours either. That the longevity of a love doesn't determine it's reality, its magnitude. And that moving on from it doesn't mean it didn't happen. That it doesn't matter. And realize, that that fact doesn't have to be something to be sorry over. That it's worth moving past. That it's okay. That it's not really anything.

That it just *is*.

24

Every Relationship You Have Is With Yourself

Brianna Wiest

It's interesting enough that human beings are the only (known) species that have relationships with themselves, but it's even more to consider the fact that human beings are the only species that have relationships with themselves *through other people.*

That is: our perceptions of other people's mindsets largely dictate how we see ourselves.

What binds us in love, in companionship, in friendship? Familiarity. The sense that you understand each other at a visceral level. It's just being able to see yourself in someone else, and more importantly, being able to change your inner-narrative when you know, see and feel that someone else loves and accepts and approves of you no matter what. Ergo: you can do the same. (It's a survival mechanism, I'm pretty sure.)

The most meaningful relationships tend to be the ones in which we're completely reflected back to ourselves because this is what relationships serve to do: open us. We only recognize this in the big, overwhelming, usually heart-wrenching ones, but it's true of *every* relationship. And it's the crux of our issues beyond basic survival: how we are in relation to other people. How we are in relation to ourselves.

The relationships we tend to be most happy in are the ones in which we adopt that other person's supposed narrative—what *we think* they think of us.

We feel most loved when we feel understood, when we are thinking that someone else is thinking in alignment with what we need to hear and believe. We feel most loved when we think someone thinks highly of us—their efforts and displays of affection serving to prove this.

This is why not just anybody can affirm for us that we're okay, only people to whom we've placed meaning. Someone to whom *we* already feel a physical or psychological connection. Someone we are looking at as a partner *for ourselves,* someone who is *like us,* someone who *understands us.*

It's why "loving yourself first" is the most common, the most confusing, and yet the most profoundly solid advice anyone can give. Because it's not really about feeling love for yourself, it's being able to feel stable enough that your mindset doesn't rest in the narrative of a supposed other's.

This is why things hurt so badly when we identify with them. All hatred is self-hatred. This is why we become so god-damned heart broken. *We cannot lose people, we can only lose ourselves in an idea of them.* We decided how we felt *about ourselves* through them—for better and for worse—so when we perceive that their mindset changes from loving us to loving someone else, our own stability goes out the window too.

The most freeing, liberating thing you can do is to realize that we are *all* a collective one and that each fragment of a bigger light refracts on one another in just a way that reveals what you need to see and understand. But that the light is always your own. Every relationship you have is with yourself. Every person in whom you feel you return "home" to is just coming back to yourself.

It's always yourself you find at the end of the journey. The sooner you face you, the less you need other people to fill voids (you cannot squeeze someone into your brokenness and expect that to make you whole.) The sooner you face you, the sooner other people's actions don't affect you negatively—your mindset doesn't depend on them. *You* don't depend on them. Relationships do not serve to give you eternal, perpetual happiness. They serve to make you more aware. The sooner you realize that said awareness is your own, the easier everything else is.

THOUGHT CATALOG Books

Thought Catalog Books is a publishing house owned by The Thought & Expression Company, an independent media group based in Brooklyn, NY. Founded in 2010, we are committed to facilitating thought and expression. We exist to help people become better communicators and listeners in order to engender a more exciting, attentive, and imaginative world.

Visit us on the web at *www.thoughtcatalogbooks.com*.

 Collective World

Thought Catalog Books is powered by Collective World, a community of creatives and writers from all over the globe. Join us at *www.collective.world* to connect with interesting people, find inspiration, and share your talent.

92932030R00057

Made in the USA
Columbia, SC
03 April 2018